Falling to Earth

by
Tom Hansen

Winner, 2005 A. Poulin, Jr. Poetry Prize
Selected by Molly Peacock

FALLING TO EARTH

Poems by
TOM HANSEN

A. POULIN, JR. NEW POETS OF AMERICA SERIES, NO. 28

BOA Editions, Ltd. ✸ Rochester, NY ✸ 2006

First Edition
06 07 08 09 10   7 6 5 4 3 2 1

Publications by BOA Editions, Ltd.—a not-for-profit corporation under section 501 (c) (3)
of the United States Internal Revenue Code—are made possible with the assistance of
grants from the Literature Program of the New York State Council on the Arts;
the Literature Program of the National Endowment for the Arts; County of Monroe, NY;
the Lannan Foundation for support of the Lannan Translation Selection Series;
Sonia Raiziss Giop Charitable Foundation; Mary S. Mulligan Charitable Trust;
Rochester Area Community Foundation; Arts & Cultural Council for Greater Rochester;
Steeple-Jack Fund; Elizabeth F. Cheney Foundation; Eastman Kodak Company;
Chesonis Family Foundation; Ames-Amzalak Memorial Trust in memory of Henry Ames,
Semon Amzalak and Dan Amzalak; and contributions from many individuals nationwide.

See Colophon on page 96 for special individual acknowledgments.

Cover Design: Geri McCormick
Cover Art: "Black Creek" by Patricia Wilder, courtesy of the artist.
Interior Design and Composition: Richard Foerster
BOA Logo: Mirko

Library of Congress Cataloging-in-Publication Data

Hansen, Tom, 1942–
  Falling to earth : poems / by Tom Hansen.— 1st ed.
    p. cm. — (A. Poulin, Jr. new poets of America series)
  ISBN 978–1–929918–75–1
  I. Title. II. Series.

PS3608.A7223F35 2006
811'.54--dc22

2005026197

BOA Editions, Ltd.
Thom Ward, Editor
David Oliveiri, Chair
A. Poulin, Jr., President & Founder (1938–1996)
260 East Avenue, Rochester, NY 14604
www.boaeditions.org

NATIONAL
ENDOWMENT
FOR THE ARTS

State of the Arts

NYSCA

for Illona

Contents

4. *Lights in the Night*

5. *Between Sleeping and Waking*

Foreword

A bemused, stoop-shouldered figure who is more than a mere speaker—let's call him a protagonist—stalks the poems of *Falling to Earth*, the book by Tom Hansen which I was honored to choose as this year's Poulin Prize winner. This protagonist calls to mind the solitary, insistent John Clare of "I Am" and the Philip Larkin of "Sad Steps" ("Groping back to bed after a piss . . ."). With candor and an almost grandiose simplicity, Hansen describes the limitations of his middle-aged body and, in doing so, the limitations of his enterprise in mid-life: the gracelessness of survival. The poet carries on a romance with the shock of the mid-life state: combining a grudging astonishment at the loss of vigor with an equally grudging astonishment that he has come this far.

Humor elbows its way through one of my favorites, "Stone. Age. Man." Here his Anglo Saxon rhythms strike against his wry weariness to make an allegorical spark:

> Hunched like a fetus,
> I lug my lover, this boulder I hug
> tight to my slack, sagging gut,
> and half stagger, stoop-shouldered
> with arm-weary bleariness,
> up the stone-cobbled slope,
> up to the slanting dirt bank,
> where I slump down to kneel,
> giving bloody hard birth to the first
> of my litter of fifty-pound rocks.

The body, unglamorous, yet still useful—or as useful as it can be before "dreaming its hundred-year sleep" as he says at the end of the poem—doggedly forges through life to give birth to a "litter of fifty-pound rocks."

The birth anchors Hansen's poetry in the aches and pains of ordinariness. Despite determination and persistence, the speaker seems surprised that he hasn't given up.

Hansen surprised me as well. When I first read *Falling to Earth*, I was moved by it, but I couldn't quite understand why. It had a musicality all its own. And like a song that seeps into you, it began to seep into me. I tried it a second time. Then I discovered his subtle instrumentation in a poem that plays with the title of the book. Here is the second stanza of "All That Fall":

> Rain fell all that fall.
> Old leaves drank it and drooled.
> Green to yellow and yellow to brown,
> they trembled, marooned in the cold.
> October had taught them black magic
> in the blood-chilling language of ice.
> Like acid, it curdled their veins
> and shriveled their rivers to rust.
> Something like steel rasped its name:
> *frost* and *frost* again *frost*.
> Why did those fools pay attention?
> But they did. They heard. They were lost.
> Down from the tree's green vision
> they tumbled. They crumbled to dust
> and disappeared into the dirt—
> like the meek, who inherit the earth.

In these rhythms I heard something of Charlotte Mew's "The Trees Are Down," ("For days there has been the grate of the saw, the swish of the branches as they fall,") and the valiant Edward Thomas, writing "Rain" ("Blessed are the dead that the rain rains upon") in the trench at Ronville in 1917. Yet why were poems of the early twentieth century in Europe evoked by Hansen's farm poems of South Dakota at the beginning of the twenty-first century? Perhaps because they share an undercurrent of threat. Casual self-interest threatens the natural world in Mew's poem, and the threat of death is palpable in Thomas' "Rain." All three poems are openly emotional. The sense of extremis leads all the poets to dispose of disguise.

What's innovative about a seemingly "plain style" poet like Hansen is that his work contains some of the roots of eco-poetry. One of the calls to the twenty-first century poet is to create awareness of the natural world—not to renew this awareness, because most people don't have the original experience of nature to be renewed. (I think of two of my friends who believed that strawberries grew underground. . . .) No, the task is to create in the reader a sense of both the brute force of growth and its fragility. Hansen provides an emotional fabric so palpable that the reader seems almost to be able to breathe inside the body of the speaker, intimately experiencing the natural world. For Hansen, falling to earth is also falling in love with it.

And this falling has a special, subtle rhythm. In "Stone. Age. Man." one hears the ghost of medieval prosody in the stressed alliteration with deep caesuras, "I lug my lover, this boulder I hug." In "All that Fall" there's a more recent measure, the trochees of "Rain fell all that fall." The music works so seductively that it almost passed through my ears without notice. Then it dawned on me that Hansen was contriving contemporary music by fertilizing the free verse with the compost of old rhythms, and the bone meal of occasional rhyme, too.

And his psychological forthrightness supplies the poems with a living fullness and flexibility. In fact, they do not seem to be art objects at all. They seem to be bodies themselves. In "I Woke Up" the speaker's mind and emotions and body all wake up as Hansen evokes the hypnogogic state:

I Woke Up

I woke up alone. All that held me down:
the warmth of my wife's arm lightly on my shoulder;
and all three dogs, curled up on the quilt
the two of us were curled up underneath . . .
And outside the window, I could hear the dead:
black, cracked corpses cackling in the yard.
Pulled so many ways, I woke up alone,
fastened by a thread to all that held me down.

The mix of the past and the present, of sleeping and waking, of being adrift and being anchored puts a terrible pressure on that thread which holds because of the verb Hansen relies on—"fastened." Hansen's world doesn't hang by a thread. It is sewn.

It may be this sense of things holding fast that lets Hansen invite terror into his work. In the midst of fear, a perspective opens, a sense of humor arrives, a perception of the weird, the weirdly true, which gives me confidence in him and lets me trust him, even when—perhaps especially when—he finds his father's head in the bathroom sink:

Father's Head

Every sunrise I wake up and yawn
and grin, *Good Morning!* to father's head.
My half-awake darling ignores me
and falls back asleep on the bed.
Before I wash or gargle or shave,
I remove father's head from the bathroom sink
and tell it a dirty joke
and give it my best left-eyed wink.
It keeps sitting there. It continues to stare,
looking at nothing, I think.

The dream made palpable without resorting to the surreal allows humor to flourish just because all the levels of human experience are acknowledged simultaneously.

How wise this poet is, I thought again and again as I reread *Falling to Earth,* awed by the ease and pith of the poems. It was easily my first choice for the Poulin Prize. No other manuscript submitted—and there were at least twenty exciting finalists—displayed such a supple flow. *Falling to Earth* is the journey of a vibrant soul refreshing itself poem by poem. *How does he make it look so easy?* I wondered. I still can't say, except that this surprising, endearing, and profound book seems to have grown from lived experience in every syllable, including these, from the last poem:

Maybe Something like This

Then one last thing, the same as the first
and so simple none of us guessed:
the world is a dream we are having together.
Each of us, lost in separate sleep,
dies a little to give the dream breath.
The shape it takes is a shape
we make with our lives.

— Molly Peacock

1. All That Fall

Stone. Age. Man.

Hunched like a fetus,
I lug my lover, this boulder I hug
tight to my slack, sagging gut,
and half stagger, stoop-shouldered
with arm-weary bleariness,
up the stone-cobbled slope,
up to the slanting dirt bank,
where I slump down to kneel,
giving bloody hard birth to the first
of my litter of fifty-pound rocks.

I rise from a tottering squat,
dripping sweat, dizzy with heat,
stumble-slide back down the slope
on legs that quiver and ache,
arrive at the rock pit, my chosen perdition,
embrace another recalcitrant lover,
and do it all over again, grunt back up—
praying like hell I don't throw out my back
or blow a rupture
or trip.

Way too ancient at fifty-six
for this kind of prison-yard labor,
but too damn-fool stubborn to stop
busting my balls bearing boulders up hill,
one heavy son at a time—
here I sit,
stone-still at sunset,
quaking arms limp at my sides,
my body a bag of bruises
dreaming its hundred-year sleep.

Garden Plot

After a day of weeding and hoeing
I feel like wilted lettuce.
Our garden is too damn big:
a giant plot to get us.

Might as well make out new wills.
Leave it to deer and rabbits.
It is not ours. We are theirs,
tending it just out of habit.

In the court of last resort
we are only migrant workers,
minions tilling the soil
for all its profligate owners.

Uprooting Weeds

I hunker down to the stem of each weed.
Choke it low. Pull on it. Slowly.
A few rise up as if out of water.
A few hold fast; then, one by one,
their subterranean fingers let go.
But most of them give no ground.

All June, these weeds have run crazy—
tortured, burning with lust,
violating the sovereign borders
of bean, tomato, zucchini,
and ravaging ancestral homelands
of acorn squash, cucumber, beet.

It will take hours crouched in the sun,
but my blade will slice down through dirt.
I will annihilate every shred
of weedy, alien growth—
and hope to sleep, this night, the sleep
of one who beat back invaders.

Under cover of darkness they strike,
hordes of green barbarians
with underworld family connections.
They sprout from the mattress, drag me away,
and leave me broken and bleeding to die
in the smoldering eye of the sun.

Men Haying

September waves roll through the meadow,
scything a whole field in one long, continuous blow.
Waist-high grass tumbles to earth, slowly rises again,
only again to be toppled by restless September wind.
Men haying far in the meadow,
        dappled in sunlight and shadow.

Grass and men and the wind insistently blowing,
distant heads bobbing, borne on those grassy waves rolling,
the meadow transformed, a watery matrix,
        a cauldron seething and bubbling,
and men haying far in the meadow,
rising and falling

and wind here-there-everywhere mowing us down
as we cradle our scythes and standing and bowing
wade through a meadow waist-deep in September
down windrows we labor our long rowing home. . . .

Systole, Diastole

In folders in files in offices
in the county courthouse in town
are pieces of paper on which we have plotted
to parcel this land among us:
Johnston and Shepard and Pentel and Williams
       and Gajdan and Darrow
            and Hansen.
My ranch. My timberland. Mine.

Deer and elk and mountain lion
and bobcat and coyote and eagle and hawk,
       attendant spirits,
             mere blood and bone,
roam this rock-ribbed hinterland
       bristling with ponderous pines
or swim shifting currents above it.
Brookies and browns and rainbows hover
in icy streams plowing through it.

And one little ember of consciousness,
       quietly fading to ash,
glides down deer trails and eases through fences
and stumbles upon a crime scene or altar.
A passionate congregation of flies
worships a carcass of wolf with no eyes.
A moldering log dreams itself green,
       far out at sea and sinking.

Fallen Apples

Wasps at work in the soft
flesh of rotting apples.
Food of the gods,
all day they mine it in
busy hushed movements.

I pick up a mushy corpse
one cold morning.
Carefully turn it over.
Its congregation tumbles
into the cupped
bowl of my hand.

Dazed, drunk, still
chilled from overnight frost,
they blunder like sleepwalkers
feeling around for lost light.
Tiny antennae test my skin
in search of something
now gone.

Warmed by my hand,
warmed by the sun,
they stagger and fall into flight,
scribble orbits
the air erases
and whine, at last, out of sight.

Old Men's Hands in Their Laps

They sit staring out from the wreckage
of mute faces—men who have lived,
whose wrinkles and scars tell tales.
Our grandfathers once, our fathers now,
and soon enough they will be us.

Dry husks that wither
in the slant light of windy October,
their final desire is to sit in the sun
and never move again—those huge hands
folded all day in their laps.

Wheat Field in Late October

Nine tall seed-heads tremble and sway,
sole survivors of drought and harvest.
They glow gold in this final moment
as sun burns down the horizon
over the white sleep of the earth.

Now they ripple and flash in the sun.
Now they flicker like nine wise tongues.
Now they bow low to the east.

Here and there, strange hieroglyphics.
Who can decipher them? What does it mean—
this dance of characters frozen in snow?
Some small scholar, inspired, bemused,
inscribed them before he passed on.

We pause, we waver, we lumber away—
tumbleweed disciples of all
the changeable gods of the winds.

Our shadows grow longer and leaner.
Flakes flash bright in the air.
Trailing behind us, a fading wake
newborn snow welcomes
but old snow forgets.

All That Fall

Rain fell all that fall.
Trunks of trees glistened black.
Old stones rose to the surface,
up from their hundred-year sleep.
A voice had spoken down deep
in the dark language of dirt—
where they waited, each one alone,
stone cold, stone deaf, stone dumb.
Something wet whispered its name:
rain and *rain* again *rain*.
How could that matter to them?
But it touched them somehow. They came.
Out of the earth's heavy dream
they eased up into the air—
a journey, at most, of inches;
an effort of long, hard years.

Rain fell all that fall.
Old leaves drank it and drooled.
Green to yellow and yellow to brown,
they trembled, marooned in the cold.
October had taught them black magic
in the blood-chilling language of ice.
Like acid, it curdled their veins
and shriveled their rivers to rust.
Something like steel rasped its name:
frost and *frost* again *frost*.
Why did those fools pay attention?
But they did. They heard. They were lost.
Down from the tree's green vision
they tumbled. They crumbled to dust
and disappeared into the dirt—
like the meek, who inherit the earth.

Rain fell all that fall.
It caressed us as much as it could—
sliding its fingers over our bodies,
trying to find a way in.
In the tentative language of touch,
it read what was etched in our skin
and it wept—for the fall of leaves,
for the resurrection of stones.
Then it made one more translation:
snow and *snow* again *snow*.
We heard that word—it crossed deserts,
claiming its own—all that fall.

As the Snow

As the snow fell faster,
trees moved away from each other,
each one marooned on its own private
　　　　island of winter.
Caught in that whirlpool, they sank at last
　　　　out of sight.

As the snow fell faster,
it came to us—we were alone:
no captain, no compass, no stars to steer by,
no one expecting to see us again
or to escort our coffin-borne
　　　　bodies back home.
The verdict was in: time to drown.

As the snow fell faster,
the world went blank. It surrendered.
At last it no longer remembered its face
　　　　or its name.

2. Going to the Dogs

Walking the Dogs in January

We stumble out into winter.
Half a foot of new snow.
It squeaks when we walk and
keeps track:
who comes and who goes and where
and whether or not they turn back.

Cold crawls up my nose.
Snakes its way down my throat.
With every breath I see
a piece of my soul leak away.
None of it ever comes back.
What if I use it all up?

But the dogs are happy,
they bound on ahead,
and what can I do but follow?
We have nowhere to go
and race through the snow
to get there as soon as we can.

When we arrive,
we will become
citizen-inmates of winter:
a country so cold only four words
of its lost language survive:
wind and *snow* and *desolation*—

and one there is no
human sound for.
Soon enough, we will be fluent
in that unspeakable tongue—
our footprints limping in circles,
dying to follow us home.

Old Dog

Old Dog goes to sleep tired
and wakes up tired from sleep.
He opens his eyes before sunrise.
The dark stares into the dark.
Ears cock forward to catch those first
faint footfalls of light.

He blinks rheum out of his eyes
and hears that familiar wheeze,
slowly stretching and limping,
waiting to get back his legs.
Then he plods out of the yard—
down to the dew-wet pasture.

Nose and eyes and pizzle-stick:
not what they should be. Or were.
All of them dribble stuff.
None of them dream any more.
But poking along through the morning,
Old Dog has his day.

Planting Poplars with Sam

Twenty-five sticks, bare roots
asleep in their dirt-filled graves,
a handful of peat moss tossed in
and water spiked
to stimulate underground dreams.
Soon buds will swell.
Fists will unfold into leaves.
In three years these trees will be
a wall of shimmering green.
Now they are skeletons leaning
away from the wind.

Sam lumbers toward me.
Her tail beats time all the way.
I still think of her as a pup:
an old one, twelve in October
if she lasts that long. But she won't.
On her belly, back near the vulva,
two lumps bulge.
Each week they grow larger,
anchored by clawlike roots and fed
by deep blue radiations
of veins.

I squat by the twenty-fifth stick.
She puts her face up to mine.
I look into dark
eyes that shine.

Chores Put Off Too Long

So many things to attend to
now it is nearly December. . . .

Six old pines lean close to the house.
Months ago they should have come down,
their bodies split and stacked: a fortress
against the fall into winter.

The water heater is clogged with rust.
Its leaky blood pools on the floor.

The choke on the '86 pickup sticks.
The engine wheezes. It rattles and sputs.

A handful of cattle have wandered off
in search of the fabled meadow.
They dream it clover sweet.
They dream June in November.

And Scout so crippled she whimpers
each time she tries to stand up. . . .

Revenant

In a pool of moonlight she lies
curled all night in new snow:
dog, wolf, old familiar
guarding the gates of our sleep.

Blue Siberian eyes
take note of our smallest gestures.
Triangular ears, cocked forward,
attend to our innermost thoughts.

One afternoon late last May
we hollowed a room in the earth
the size of her cedar-filled bed
and welcomed her home.

How many nights since then
have we heard her come and go,
prowling the borders of dreams,
howling out there in the snow?

Night Shift

Sitting here in the dark before daylight
next to the husky lying beside me,
waiting for nothing,
for stars to move when we don't look—
we bow our heads
and close our eyes to help them
on their blind way,

and for once I am happy to know
I am only a beast who will die
on a night like this
when the world lies asleep
while we wait under stars with no names
for something to break.
Maybe it will be day.

Old Campfire Story

They found him after that five-day blow.
    Naked. Out by the fence line.
Saw what they took for a timber wolf—
head on the snow, between two huge paws—
    holding its ground as they came.
They thought: maybe hurt, maybe hording a kill.
    Then they edged closer and saw.
Must have been crazy or drunk, they said.
    Nothing else could explain.

It was him, all right. Flat on his back.
    Skin stretched tight over bone.
Clothes all folded. Stacked there beside him.
Eyes open, staring straight up. At what?
    One of them swore he was smiling.
The only prints in the snow: his own,
    except for those pawprints, of course.
The dog slunk away. Who knows where?
    But some nights you hear a far howling.

Scars Rising out of Old Snow

The footprints, the pawprints,
the faint stain of blood.
They fade so slowly. It takes forever.
We wake up one day. They are gone.

All our footprints and pawprints
and bloodprints—
rising up out of old snow melting
and silently walking away.

3. Water Striders

Crying Uncle

1

Uncle Fred never gave up.
He stood out there in the rain all day long,
biding his own sweet time,
casting and reeling in, cold to the bones,
waiting for that old lunker smallmouth to strike.

Twice before, he had hooked Beelzebub,
feeling the line all at once jerk tight
while the rod went crazy and tried to jump in the lake.
Then, when it was already too late,
had witnessed something like fury

come boiling up to the surface,
twisting and thrashing in great fish convulsions,
fighting the thing that dragged him toward shore.
In one last leap, he spit out the hook
and fell back to the black cathedral of water.

The most Uncle Fred ever caught of him
was a shred of ripped lip he kept in a sinker box.
Said if he had to, he'd catch that damn fish
a chunk at a time—and put it together
piece by piece like a jigsaw puzzle, by God.

Each time out, before the first cast,
he shook that box to make the lip rattle
and shouted out over the water,
"Here's a hunk of your lip, Old Fish.
Now I've come back for the rest!"

2

The last time I saw him alive
was flat on his back between heart attacks
in the Edmore Memorial Hospital.
He pulled at the line that came out of his chest
and begged me to cut him loose.

He reached for his needle-nosed pliers and cried,
"Tommy Boy, there's a hook in my heart,"
and if only I could wiggle it free,
he could head for the drop-off and hide
below the dark, brooding lake.

He thrashed and twisted and cried out in horror
at sheets brown with mud in his bed made of water.
Then his keepers came running and held him down
and pumped him to sleep with a needle.
I watched and waited.

He was out at the lake one last time,
gulping air like a fish out of water,
staring hard at something that I couldn't see.
Then he slumped down into his bed and whimpered
and slowly sank out of sight.

Keeping Your Head Above Water

Nothing in sight means nothing to swim toward.
In that case, your job is to stay alive as long as you possibly can.
Swimming is suicide. Every movement is lost strength,
and strength is your weapon. Instead, lie back. Stretch your arms.
Pretend you are being crucified. Close your eyes and let your legs sink
until you are floating standing in water.
This is called the dead float. In quiet water you can maintain it
for days if nothing happens.

Forget about sharks or bad weather or falling asleep.
Whatever comes, if it comes, will probably kill you,
but what can you do? Keep your head above water.
Dead float as long as you can.

In two days the salt will dehydrate your skin.
Thirst will wring you out, but drinking the sea will kill you.
Drink the rain if it rains, or bite your lip and drink blood.
But remember what sunlight and salt will do
to your broken mouth. Remember the scent of your blood
lures love-starved sharks.

After four days of the dead float, the sun will burn out your eyes.
By then you will have seen too much—touched by the sea
in a way that will make you different from anything human.

If, before blindness, you sight in the distance land or a ship or
some floating object, go slowly. Teach your heart to be still.
Speed is your enemy. Hope is your enemy. Teach yourself
to take time. The secret of long-distance swimming is resting
between every slow, easy stroke.

Never wear yourself out. Never think you are almost there.
You are never almost there until you are there.

Rain Song

It was the rain again,
bang against the window:
communion of suicides
oozing down the glass.
What did the rain say,
blind in its nightfall?—
sinners in the wind, oh,
stations of our loss?

Strange journey down,
sang the little globules,
whipped by the wind
in a dream of immolation.
Father Drip and Mother Drop,
blessed be your drowning—
all your sons and daughters,
commingling in the dark.

O Jesus of the rock-wrecked,
crawl upon these waters.
Be the buoy we cling to,
cold and pale and sinking.
The great wind takes us,
bubbles on the surface.
Something comes to wake us.
Strange journey down.

The Woman Who Fell in Love with Water

The woman who fell in love with water
fell in.
Each time she leaned over,
that dark other rising to meet her:
green silence, lip to watery lip.
She who had nothing gave herself
to the perfect embrace of water.

We who never go deeper than mirrors—
our rooms grow small. They cannot contain
someone waiting to name us,
whose voice we do not hear.
But the woman who fell in love with water
listened.
She heard green silence.

O woman in water, always I see
the punished fingers of your hair
and feel the current gentle you on your way.
Slowly, my body bending over your body,
I come to drink.
Between sleeping and waking. In green silence.
Where falling and rising are one.

Return

We have dreamed they are real: mermaids,
breathtaking creatures with breasts and fish tails
and long lovely arms to encircle us
and drag us down to their wild beds of weeds
where they gaze as sunlight and shadow
dapple our pale perfect beauty.
Their fervent fingers bless our bodies:
our hair teased by amorous currents,
our foreheads so smooth and untroubled,
the hollows, rondures, and gentle slopes
of our faces, those maps of our lives.

They look so long and so deep
into windows that once were our eyes
and sigh at the sad unresponsiveness
of our delicate, blue-tinged lips.

Then shoulder to breastbone to belly,
exploring the subtle way down,
they arrive at our odd nether parts.
The first is a short one-eyed eel
swaying in front of two stones in a bag.
They look and touch. They touch and wonder.
Then they move on to those strange formations:
tapering columns, long useless hands
cursed with blunt mutant fingers. How sad.

Some nights it happens. We just drift away
from the beds of our last earthly spouses.
They weep invisible tears. Tear their hair.
Then they find us and tow us back home.

At last they notice. We never eat.
Yet our poor bodies bulge day by day
as we turn into fat little Buddhas
who now and then like to feed fishes.
O how their cold-blooded hearts just melt
as we tender our succulent morsels
to their countless ravenous cousins.

And we—will we know? Will we see?
Will we feel those gentle caresses?
Will we weep, "After all these years,
the love of my life—here at last"?

Under Water

I, who lied to so many in bed,
toss and turn in the bed of the river.
Turtles dine on my wide, vacant eyes.
Minnows softly explore the curious
O-shaped cave of my mouth.

My tongue, so practiced in cunning tricks,
is dumb stone in a tomb. My fingers,
those wizards at buttons and zippers,
can undo nothing. Least of all this.
My bones grow stiff. All but one.

My body is all done with doing.
It lives in a world of slow nudgings:
lazy current's whispered urging,
underwater branches clutching,
little wrigglers busy nibbling, nuzzling.

X at Sea

X woke up on a ship.
Seems to be the only one
who doesn't know what for. Or where.
But late at night X lies awake.
Feels the steady pulse propelling
X the Silly, X the Sane,
X the Craven, X the Brave,
and all the other X's
       through the dark.

The others say, *Relax. Enjoy.*
They skim the surface: never ask
what depths there are to plumb,
cannot fathom where the little
bubble rises from—
or why it tries so hard to break
the holy law of gravity,
climbing blindly upward
       toward the light.

A Little Meditation on a Bubble

What is the meaning of a bubble from the bottom of the sea?
—Joseph Campbell

To comprehend the meaning of a bubble, one has to imagine the unimaginable: a fathomless blackness of water (the Void, the Facelessness, the great Before—as it is variously known in the evocative nomenclature of bubble-ology) out of which a fragile something, which before was nothing, comes. A little sphericule of air issues thence. It rises up. It is surpassingly ascendent. Mindless nature names it Wanderer and drives it on.

So it is that into a shadowy, watery place—*into* this world, yet not wholly *of* it—something arrives: unicellular animalcule, pulsing piece of protoplasm, gob of bubble spit wrapped in sticky skin. Little Homunculus, Baby Bubblekins—caught in time's labyrinth; armless, legless, useless. A little birth-to-be. A little death beyond. It rises up. Surpassingly ascendent.

Certain scholars theorize that bubbles are phototropic: germinating in darkness and climbing up toward light. Those who subscribe to vitalist notions even insist that bubbles have rudimentary souls; that the sun is a bright, shiny god in their inarticulate mythology; that dim intimations of immortality urge them to seek union with this glory. This, say mythographers of bubbledom, explains the life cycle of a bubble. Ever yearning heavenward, it seeks to break beyond the bounds of nature. And then, at last, the pilgrimage of bubbles leads them to that membrane separating this world from the next. But the airy world of sunlight is too much for them to bear. Their poor hearts burst in ecstasy. Thus they break free. Their disembodied souls become one with that oceanic other known as air. It receives them to its bosom.

Such accounts of the inner life of bubbles are compelling. One wishes they were also true. But for truth—which is seldom as engaging as a rousing theory uncontaminated by brute facts—for truth, one must turn to the biophysicists. Yes, they agree, bubbles rise toward the sun. They also rise toward the moon and on moonless nights toward stars and on starless nights toward the great dark above, whose image mirrors that of the great dark below, from which bubbles come. The only constant here, insist the biophysicists, is this: bubbles rise. The simple explanation: specific gravity. They have no souls. They are only things. The universe itself is only a machine—a very intricate machine—working through its labyrinthine, intersecting cycles.

Bubbles do what bubbles do because of what they are. Their bodies are the key to their destiny. The matrix out of which they come is dense beyond imagining: hundreds of pounds of pressure per square inch. Surrounded by this immensity of density, a bubble is compacted. Its molecules huddle tight together. Its heartbeat slows. Seeking equilibrium, as all things do, it rises through the birth canal toward water above, whose density is less than that of water below. Perhaps on its upward journey, it nearly knocks heads with a stone tumbling toward the bottom—another Wanderer in search of equilibrium.

So the little bubble rises, slowly growing larger as the upper water, into which it now ascends, bears less and less of the weight of the ocean on its shoulders. At last, it attains the empyrean of water and discovers itself on the floor of yet another ocean: the fathomless and insubstantial air. Having transcended that vast, murky matrix, the whole immense heft of which now buoys it up, it bobs on the surface in its moment in the sun, waiting for its filmy membrane to burst, waiting to be thrust into a subtler incarnation. . . .

At this precise point, biophysics falls mute—the bubble having, after all, ceased to be a bubble.

What, then, is the meaning of a bubble from the bottom of the sea?

Perhaps it *means* nothing because it *is* nothing: a substanceless little something passing through the world on its way to a nowhere much like that from which it came. And the world itself is none the wiser for the bubble's having been; in which case, one might claim, it has *not* been. Between its entrance and its exit is a brief career: its life no different from the life of any of its species. Or of any other species. A bubble, after all, being nothing, is nothing more and nothing less than anything: a cloud, a stone, a drop of rain, a grain of sand, a continent, an ocean, a speck of cosmic dust adrift in cosmic space. A universe.

None survives its moment. All ripen toward perfection, then hasten to decay.

And if, as some have said, microcosm mirrors macrocosm, the universe itself is just a bubble ballooning ever outward into emptiness. But if, as others say, it has no membrane, perhaps it is a just-burst bubble—

fragments blasting outward from what once had been its heart. And we, the subatomic, all-but-conscious aborigines of a minor microfragment of this just-burst bubble—we say this is *the* universe. As if the timeless depth of time belched forth but one small sphere of gas. As if this one small belch were The Creation. As if there were no others. . . .

As if we could unravel the meaning of a bubble. As if we could travel to the bottom of the sea and see it for ourselves and feel it bubbling in our blood—and shudder in a shock of recognition: *we came that way, too.* This house of water once was ours. One day we left home, taking pieces of it with us, in us—little globules locked inside each cell of blood and brain and bone. We are inland seas, nomadic oceans, bags of water rising up. Surpassingly ascendent. Something bubbles in us, seeking equilibrium. Up from the dark below we fall, tumbling toward the dark above. Lighted by a little dark within.

Jump-Rope Rhyme

Tat tvam asi:
thou art *that*—
that leaf, that tree,
that cow, that cat,
that cloud, that sky,
that moon, that sun,
that *you*, that *I*—
for all are one.
So here you are
but there you go
and who you were
you hardly know.

I think this *I*
is only *me*:
a drip, a drop,
but not the sea.
Yet when I wake
from these brief dreams,
then like the snake
I'll shed what seems:
this mask, this skin,
this ball and chain.
I will begin
to fall like rain.

Our heart's last home:
the wind-whipped foam,
the sweet, deep sea.
Tat tvam asi.

In the Home for Rudderless Derelicts

1

This fishy smelling bed is the rock
his life has shipwrecked on.
He boards it at sunset these days
when the halls start to pitch and roll.
But safely stowed in the hold,
he squints his eyes to a slit,
looses his hawser, hoists his halyard,
and, easing into the briny mattress,
feels the shore slip away.
Soon enough, he is lost, at sea—
scudding before a stiff sou-wester,
splattered with salt sea spray.

2

Sinbad, marooned in bed,
how can you be
so far from shore?
What do you see?

What bright beings
attend your delirium?
What beasties rise
from the murky mysterium
this night of all dark
nights of your soul,
old salt hellbent
for death's wet hole?

3

    then rolls over
    opens his eyes
    piss-warm pajamas
    cling to his thighs

And faint, sweet smell of shit
and enduring scent of decay
on flesh not washed this day.

    then looking down
    perched atopmast
    white coats pounding
    an old man's chest

Swarm about him mad to touch him
and mutter arcane incantations
and wait for what comes.

    then a great wave
    caves in the hull
    lungs gargle blood
    leaky bulkheads fill

Rung by rung, up Jacob's ladder,
into the waiting embrace of water,
the sinking pilot ascends.

    comes to an end
    continues to be
    now he has boarded
    the wide windy sea

Once Below Time

I would like to think
it still exists:
Atlantis, Avalon, Eden—
that mythical kingdom where
time stands still,
holding its breath,
slowly counting from one
down to nothing—

a land below waves,
always just
beyond the setting sun,
where the moon is large and full
of unspoken promise,
where our little boat
goes from great deep
to great deep.

Let us set sail
while there is still
good wind—
across the gulf that leads
to the edge of the world.
Perhaps we will drown
or grow too old to dream.
Or come to ourselves
or not. . . .

4. Lights in the Night

The Plot Thickens

A shot rings out,
fatally wounding the dark.

It pricks a hole in the bowl
of the cranial vault.

A trickle of orphaned light
leaks from the stars.

In the Clearing

At twenty-four you are the most gentle
dangerous person I know. Do I?
What can I say you can hear?
All my scars are inside:
the compromises of middle age.
Things I don't want to
but can't afford not to
I do.

That's how I got where I am:
here in the clearing. But you
got here by ways I don't know.
Do I want to?
The crescent moon hangs by a thread.
We must beware: not to stray
into shadows—to stay
in the clearing.

The fire between us is embers
breathed back to life.
A cold hungry wind snakes its way
down our necks.
In a scatter of ashes and sparks
by firelight by moonlight I see it.
Across your throat—Jesus!—
I see it.

Things I want to ask
you won't answer.
*How far can a body fall
before it grows bloodstained wings?
Are we falling or flying? Is dying
the only way home?*

Things I don't ask you
don't answer.

Moon Music

Moonlight pours through the open window.
Music streams out—into the wide
net of night.
Soon this room will be filled with nothing
but moonlight, the perfect music
of silence,
and soon the night on the side of the window
filled with the singing absence
of moon
will feel its body rise and grow luminous,
riding that river of black
Rachmaninoff blood.

Moonsongs

1. Alone All Day on His Birthday
  He Wades Outside at Midnight
    to Greet an Old Friend

Between the full moon and me they lean,
a stand of old ponderosa.
Pale rays filter through tangled branches.

I stare at that watery face looking down.
Shattered light spatters my eyes.
I surrender. Or drown. Or become
something more, or less—someone other:
a patchwork of shadow and glimmer
marooned on a seascape of snow,
a mottled manshape of fragments
alone on a dim ocean floor.

My luminous body, giddy on moonshine,
begins to sway to a faraway music
this fifty-fourth year of my birth.

2. The Bars on His Windows So Many
  Nothing Escapes but These Words

The moon does not know He is God.
That is my job. To watch Him. To know.
He is tied up—*Down with ebb! Up with flood!*—
doing His moon job come day-bright or night-dim.
He is The Main Cheese, The Man in The Moon,
a big chunk of cheddar or Swiss, I guess,
high in the sky, all but full, all but gone,
but still The One, The Moon, The Moon,
pale and pock-marked and dressed up in stripes.

Here in my chair, I sit and sigh
while distant lights in the sky wheel by
and leaves whirl past as they fall through October.
I hear their corpses cackle and whisper.
Not one will survive.
Not one will return.
But The Moon, The Moon, The Moon, The Moon:
It will rise and fall and die and be born.
I watch. I wait. By cold light I burn.

3. Loony Tune

Full moon, gibbous moon, half moon,
horned moon, no moon, new moon—

moon that wanders the star-riddled sky
in search of a place to lie down,
moon that shrivels to nothing and dies
and comes back in three days' time,

moon that remembers the lost way home
and the secret history of dreams,
moon that knows what we were called
before we got born and wore names,

O dim companion, piece of green cheese,
queen of heaven, ship on high seas,
Astarte, Phoebe, Diana, Cynthia,
Artemis, Hecate, Selene, Amarynthia,

demi-lune, pleni-lune, falling and rising,
I lie here below you, drowsing and rousing,
rinsed by your soft silky light
shed in the sweet dead of night.

4. Return

On my long journey back
to the kingdom of sleep
feathers fell out of my wings,
my flippers became hands and feet,
leaf, limb, and root
fell to rot, fell to blight.

When I arrived I found myself
floating face downward in bed.
I huddled as close as I could
to that body.
O Moon, I prayed, *give me
permission to drown.*

5. Moonset

This morning at five I stood at the window
and stared at the great blind eye of the moon.
It navigated its tangled way
through branches of tall ponderosa,
easing down toward the western horizon
less than an hour before dawn.

A congregation of coyotes howled,
an old man's heart lurched in my chest,
and a fine tremor danced through his fingers,
inscribing invisible words on the air.

I watched and waited. The sky grew pale.
The old moon faded and slowly fell.
It disappeared in a thicket of pines.
I think it is hiding there still.

The Moon. The Moon. The Moon.

1

Lips crinkle into an O.
Hole of the throat opens up.
Feathery lungs beat like wings
in the sweet, autistic dark.

How many times can we say its name
before this enchantment dissolves?
How many moans before
our ghost returns to his chains?

2

When it rains all night, every night,
first we miss the moon,
then we worry about the moon,
and at last we find
we have lost our faith.
Was there ever a moon?

We hear earth heave a sigh
as rain bleeds into its wounds.
We rise and walk in sleep
and go in search of the moon.

We fear the moon is sick
or its life is no longer its own
or it is dying to tell us something
we are not dying to hear.

3

It is too late.
We have murdered the moon.
All we have said about it
shows how little we know—
making it bear the weight
of all our losses and loves.

We must be honest for once
about the moon and us.

The moon does not reflect upon us
light sent by the sun.
We reflect upon it
whatever dim light we have.
The moon is not inconstant.
We are inconstant
to it and ourselves.
The moon does not die
and get born.
We are the ones
who must learn.

If only we could be alone
all night
in the kingdom of moon;
if only, robed in its light,
we could let go
of all we know;
if only we could hear in our sleep
its lovely lunatic song,
perhaps at last
we would wake up to the moon.

4

What I think some nights,
when I see broken pieces of moon
shimmer on top of water
disturbed by wind,

is that we are water
disturbed by wind,
or we are pieces of moon,
or, living between two worlds,

we are some kind of shimmering thing.

Riding at Night

Bareback on broken-down horses,
we plod through the woods in December.
Our lives become what they must become:
snow dust and moon shadow,
restless west wind.

Midnight Ponderosa

Shadowy pines plunge leeward,
seized by gods we call winds,
waving wild arms at the sky,
whose pale, blind eye peers down.

Countdown

See these last few candles flicker.
One by one the stars burn out.
All around us darkness deepens.
Little winding path. Big night.

Full Moon

How many times before, old friend,
playing at this game,
have you and I stood face to face
with miles of dark between?

Not once, I think, but many times
in many different times and places
you and I with different names
faced the night with different faces,

never, in all those times, aware
of any time except our own—
as if this game of who we are
were tied to where or when. . . .

5. Between Sleeping and Waking

Nightwalker

Long past dark, after the windows
        one by one close their eyes
and the house floats away, rocked in the arms
        of its dreams,
the walker comes striding over
        the face of the watery deep.
His footsteps leave moon-wrinkled scars.
        They shimmer. They heal.

They circle the house behind him,
        stopping before each window.
He peers into rooms where our bodies
        lie in the dark wrapped in sheets.
What sings, what flickers, what burns, he wonders,
        in these cocoons?
Again and again around the house
        he walks and pauses and looks.

Sleeper

It is mid-morning. Without waking up
I am aware of a man on the edge of my bed.
Sunlight breaks through the window,
creeps down the bedspread.
When it reaches the floor at last
it will pause. It will take a deep breath,
then slowly crawl back to the window.
I dream these things but have no idea
I am asleep and dreaming.

The man who sits on my bed is still waiting.
He must have something important to tell me.
He is the soul of patience itself
for now it is late afternoon.
Sunlight through the opposite window
journeys across the floor
to the side of my bed it will climb to whisper
secret things in my ear.
I force myself to lie still.

Then I dream I wake up.
I dream I forget all these things.
A door locks behind me. Who holds the key?
Why can't I find it? Where could it be?
I sit on the edge of the bed.
I look at my hands. No key.
I know it is somewhere near. So I sit
drifting in waters between little islands of thought.
This continues.

Something distracts me. Sunlight.
I watch it flow down the bedspread.
Have I been sitting here thinking all night?
All at once I am aware of a man

sleeping in this very bed,
disturbed by this very same dream.
He will wake up. Soon I hope.
When he does I will ask him, *Where is the key?*
Until then I must be patient.

I Woke Up

I woke up alone. All that held me down:
the warmth of my wife's arm lightly on my shoulder;
and all three dogs, curled up on the quilt
the two of us were curled up underneath;
and downstairs on my desk, a little pile of mail
a long thin blade would soon persuade to spill its
      crisp, white guts:
a few amazing offers, a wedding invitation,
a plea from yet one more lost cause, a bill or two
      long overdue. . . .
And outside the window, I could hear the dead:
black, cracked corpses cackling in the yard.
Pulled so many ways, I woke up alone,
fastened by a thread to all that held me down.

I woke up lost, the day laid out before me
and next to it, its twins, the days before and after:
a never-ending busyness of interlocking circles
my bare feet hit the cold wood floor already
      dumbly dancing,
as if they knew the way—as if there *were* a way.
Jesus said He was The Way. Which way did He go?
The only path He left: a fading wake on water.
So there was none—no way, except that crooked
      trail I plowed,
trough to peak to trough, looking for another.

I woke up thirsty, roaring for a drink,
and saw the bed was empty, the dogs long gone,
the mailbox gorged and throwing up TO WHOM
      and OCCUPANT,
the trees bored stiff with their old arthritic pose,
the grave yard scarred with drifts of sickly snow,
the morning sky laid out in mourning gray.

I woke up dazed and shaky, holding out my glass,
wading through the desert while I prayed for rain
     , or bourbon.
God heard my plea and filled my glass with sand.
I stand here slowly sinking—his answer in my hand.

Flutes and Bones

One day it begins, an envelope comes.
The name, not yours, not anyone's name.
There is no return address,
the mailman says it is out of his hands,
and no one will pick the damn thing up
where you leave it lying for days
on the sidewalk.
The heavy air, closing in.
Flutes and bones, the old sounds.

Two weeks and the ink is dry,
you have legally changed your name.
Now you are someone who never was
and he is you and the letter is his.
One deep breath and you open it.
Waiting inside, this message:
Rejoice, for today is the day
the dead man with an erection
will point the way.

Too late to sell all your clothes.
You are already naked and nowhere.
The snow is deep, the wind
can't seem to make up its mind,
the great stones they call stars
burn holes through the night.
All the lines of your life converge
into one fixed point. You carry it,
a wound in the palm of your hand.

Flutes and bones, oldest of sounds,
rising from underground caves—
and the silence of someone naked
who tiptoes out into snow.

His is a blind hunter, his penance
is tracking white mice in winter.
Darkness his light, his fingers listen
and follow the mouse-foot syllables home.
Oldest of sounds. Flutes and bones.

Journey

It will be morning the day you set out
across a sea of sand,
the usual unreliable maps
carved in the palms of your hands,
your only trustworthy guide
a wind-blasted trail of bleached bones.

When in the shimmering distance you see
a lake receding before you,
an ocotillo, its blood-spattered arms
erasing illegible words from the air,
a palo verde chained to the bed
of a river that dried up and died—

when you read these omens
believe what they say and believe
the silence beneath what they say
about the other world hidden in this world,
about the great blind eye of God,
that terrible madness, that love.

Expect no rejoicing when you arrive.
The gates of the city will shriek
in the arms of their hinges of rust.
You will be made to submit
to lizard, to coyote, to snake:
priests of this burning sanctum.

The sun will tool your skin.
You will be robed in etched leather—
a desert creature whose face, whose eyes
tell tales that lie where words fail.
All this will cost you the rest of your life.
Fall on your knees. Weep. Give thanks.

The Land of Watery Dark

I was nearly fifty when it happened.
The path, which had always warned itself
to keep away from the forest,
suddenly surrendered. Its molecules sang.
Come, little brother, it crooned
and plunged in and drowned.

I stood there for nine months waiting,
but my map refused to name names.
That silence told me
this was the edge of the world.
I knew it was time. I knew
I had no choice. I was free.

I followed the path into the forest,
into the land of watery dark, the heart's home,
where streams are born dreaming
their long, winding way to the sea.
Come, little brothers and sisters.
Drink this wine. Sing this song.

Waking to Sleep

Each dreams only what is appropriate to his own metaphysical guidance.
—Schopenhauer

I dream I am forty-two again,
leaner and more alert than ever,
a man who lies awake at night
washed in a sea of sounds:
what the night wind says
testing windows and doors,
how our old house creaks
sinking into the earth,
why dogs bark this dark night
at shadows they see every night,
and where she is now,
whose breathing I no longer hear.

I catch each sound, far or near,
until there is nothing else:
wave upon wave upon wave
tossing my rudderless boat—
the dim, inexplicable music
random night-noises make. . . .

I dream I wake before dawn
to see another day born—
the only one awake in a house
where others asleep still dream:
a naked, yawning apparition
eager to live one more time.

I dream I am happily doomed,
marooned on this little
island of blossoming silence
with no hope of rescue,

not for an hour or two.
Then in the distance, a ship
manned by two boys with a dog
and captained by a woman
I recall as if from a dream.
They talk and bark
and bang things about
and start frying bacon and eggs.

They grapple my waterlogged carcass,
haul it aboard each morning,
revive me and teach me their language.

Some Numbers

0

I see you gone from where
you never were.
Your absence blossoms,
present everywhere
as if it were the air.
Nought and ought,
you are the none.
Your all is less
than even one.
Round and shining
like the sun
and self-contained—
and you are gone.

1

And who are you?
Ah, yes—I know.
You are the one
one more than none,
from which all comes.
You are the source,
the primal force,
the unseen face—
of her, of course:
both womb and tomb
and witch and lover,
whose flesh we break—
our sacred mother.

2

And now, let's see. . . .
Who might you be?
I ought to know
the likes of you.
You are the one.
You are the two.
You are the father
and the son,
the rust-red tree
the fruit hangs on.
The ripe-sweet fruit,
the blood-smeared tree—
all this I see.

3

I look again.
How can this be?
You were just two
and now are three:
a stone, a stream,
a budding tree—
what was, what is,
and what will be.
What is once was
what was to be.
So all are one
and one is three.
Makes sense to me!

4

Each time I look
I find one more.
I turn around
and you are four.
The right hand, east:
my rising sun.
The left hand, west:
one more day done.
North: sky above,
so far away.
South: earth below,
where I must stay—
to teach myself
what numbers say.

Father's Head

Every sunrise I wake up and yawn
and grin, *Good Morning!* to father's head.
My half-awake darling ignores me
and falls back asleep on the bed.
Before I wash or gargle or shave,
I remove father's head from the bathroom sink
and tell it a dirty joke
and give it my best left-eyed wink.
It keeps sitting there. It continues to stare,
looking at nothing, I think.

Every day I walk home from work
in order to give father's head some fresh air.
Sometimes we go to the graveyard
to find out if mother's still there.
Other times we stroll through the park
where the children of darkness work at play,
blind and crippled and mindless.
O Head of My Father, I say,
These broken ones, your daughters and sons—
why did God make them that way?

Every midnight I sit down to think
(confusions and questions and father's old head)
and think of my half-asleep darling
alone on her half of the bed
and think of mother buried out there
and think of the children of darkness and think
of father's head and of me—
and sit and continue to think. . . .
My eyes run red. I put father's head
back in the bathroom sink.

The Dance

I danced with the question Why.
She kissed me on the nose.
I pressed her to my chest and felt
her heartbeat through my clothes.
And then before I knew it I
was dancing with Suppose.

Suppose had big blue eyes.
She lightly held my paws.
We whirled about the ballroom floor
to waves of wild applause.
I drank her warmth, inhaled her sighs,
and then I saw Because.

Because was like bright light.
Her beauty scorched my eyes.
I turned away my face and learned
to love the sunless sky.
I stood beneath the starry night,
the reason being Why.

Maybe Something like This

Wake up slowly, open our eyes,
and see the world isn't ours.
Tell ourselves (because in a dream
we keep repeating, *It's only a dream*)
the same thing over and over:
This is the one I was born to live.
And then go into it deep.

Let things happen however they will.
They will. They don't need our approval.
We are part of something big going on,
but we ourselves are not big.
Still, we are here, everywhere in it,
watching it happen and being what happens,
trying to find out its name.

Then one last thing, the same as the first
and so simple none of us guessed:
the world is a dream we are having together.
Each of us, lost in separate sleep,
dies a little to give the dream breath.
The shape it takes is a shape
we make with our lives.

Acknowledgments

Grateful acknowledgment is made to the following publications, where these poems first appeared, often in altered versions and sometimes with different titles:

Anima: "A Little Meditation on a Bubble" and "Once Below Time";
Bitter Oleander: "Night Shift";
The CEA Critic: "The Land of Watery Dark";
Confrontation: "Old Campfire Story";
The Florida Review: "X at Sea";
Greenfield Review: "Keeping Your Head Above Water";
Images: "Waking to Sleep";
Indefinite Space: "The Plot Thickens";
Kansas Quarterly: "Father's Head";
Lake Effect: "All That Fall";
The Midwest Quarterly: "Sleeper";
The Northern Centinel: "The Moon. The Moon. The Moon.";
Phi Kappa Phi Forum: "Old Dog";
Poetry Northwest: "Crying Uncle," "Rain Song" and "The Woman Who Fell in Love with Water";
Poetry Now: "The Dance";
Prime Times: "Maybe Something like This";
The Smith: "Flutes and Bones";
Southern Poetry Review: "Moon Music" and "Planting Poplars with Sam";
The Sun: "Jump-Rope Rhyme" and "Some Numbers";
Weber Studies: "Walking the Dogs in January";
Whiskey Island Magazine: "In the Home for Rudderless Derelicts."

"Old Men's Hands in Their Laps" appeared in the anthology *As Far as I Can See,* edited by Charles L. Woodard and published by Windflower Press in 1989.

Two artist fellowship grants from the South Dakota Arts Council allowed me to complete some of these poems.

Thanks to Glenessence and to the Ragdale Foundation for periods of residence during which some of these poems were written.

Thanks to Molly Peacock for selecting *Falling to Earth* as winner of the 2005 A. Poulin, Jr. Poetry Prize.

About the Author

Tom Hansen taught writing and literature courses for thirty-five years at Northern State University in South Dakota before retiring to the Black Hills, where he lives on ten acres of hilly, rocky, ponderosa-covered land with his wife, their husky, an indeterminate number of deer and wild turkeys, and, now and then, a vagrant mountain lion. Over the past quarter century, his poems, essays, and reviews have appeared in *The Literary Review*, *The Midwest Quarterly*, *New York Quarterly*, *Poetry Northwest*, *Rattle*, *Southern Poetry Review*, *The Sun*, *Tar River Poetry*, *Weber Studies*, and numerous other journals and occasional anthologies.

BOA Editions, Ltd.

THE A. POULIN, JR. NEW POETS OF AMERICA SERIES

No. 1   *Cedarhome*
         Poems by Barton Sutter
         Foreword by W.D. Snodgrass

No. 2   *Beast Is a Wolf with Brown Fire*
         Poems by Barry Wallenstein
         Foreword by M.L. Rosenthal

No. 3   *Along the Dark Shore*
         Poems by Edward Byrne
         Foreword by John Ashbery

No. 4   *Anchor Dragging*
         Poems by Anthony Piccione
         Foreword by Archibald MacLeish

No. 5   *Eggs in the Lake*
         Poems by Daniela Gioseffi
         Foreword by John Logan

No. 6   *Moving the House*
         Poems by Ingrid Wendt
         Foreword by William Stafford

No. 7   *Whomp and Moonshiver*
         Poems by Thomas Whitbread
         Foreword by Richard Wilbur

No. 8   *Where We Live*
         Poems by Peter Makuck
         Foreword by Louis Simpson

No. 9   *Rose*
         Poems by Li-Young Lee
         Foreword by Gerald Stern

No. 10   *Genesis*
         Poems by Emanuel di Pasquale
         Foreword by X.J. Kennedy

No. 11   *Borders*
         Poems by Mary Crow
         Foreword by David Ignatow

No. 12   *Awake*
         Poems by Dorianne Laux
         Foreword by Philip Levine

No. 13   *Hurricane Walk*
         Poems by Diann Blakely Shoaf
         Foreword by William Matthews

No. 14   *The Philosopher's Club*
         Poems by Kim Addonizio
         Foreword by Gerald Stern

No. 15   *Bell 8*
         Poems by Rick Lyon
         Foreword by C. K. Williams

No. 16   *Bruise Theory*
         Poems by Natalie Kenvin
         Foreword by Carolyn Forché

No. 17   *Shattering Air*
         Poems by David Biespiel
         Foreword by Stanley Plumly

No. 18   *The Hour Between Dog and Wolf*
         Poems by Laure-Anne Bosselaar
         Foreword by Charles Simic

No. 19   *News of Home*
         Poems by Debra Kang Dean
         Foreword by Colette Inez

No. 20   *Meteorology*
         Poems by Alpay Ulku
         Foreword by Yusef Komunyakaa

No. 21   *The Daughters of Discordia*
         Poems by Suzanne Owens
         Foreword by Denise Duhamel

No. 22   *Rare Earths*
         Poems by Deena Linett
         Foreword by Molly Peacock

No. 23   *An Unkindness of Ravens*
         Poems by Meg Kearney
         Foreword by Donald Hall

No. 24   *Hunting Down the Monk*
         Poems by Adrie Kusserow
         Foreword by Karen Swenson

No. 25   *Big Back Yard*
         Poems by Michael Teig
         Foreword by Stephen Dobyns

No. 26   *Elegy with a Glass of Whiskey*
         Poems by Crystal Bacon
         Foreword by Stephen Dunn

No. 27   *The Eclipses*
         Poems by David Woo
         Selected by Michael S. Harper

No. 28   *Falling to Earth*
         Poems by Tom Hansen
         Foreword by Molly Peacock

Colophon

Falling to Earth, poems by Tom Hansen,
is set in Monotype Dante with text design
by Richard Foerster, York Beach, Maine.
The cover design is by Geri McCormick.
The cover art, "Black Creek" by Patricia Wilder,
is courtesy of the artist.
Manufacturing is by McNaughton & Gunn, Lithographers,
Saline Michigan.

❄

The publication of this book is made possible, in part,
by the special support of the following individuals:

Lawrence Belle & Bernadette Reidy
Alan & Nancy Cameros
Craig Challender ❄ Gwen & Gary Conners
Peter & Suzanne Durant
Bev & Pete French
Jack & Bonnie Garner
Dane & Judy Gordon
Kip & Deb Hale
Peter & Robin Hursh ❄ Robert & Willy Hursh
Juliet & Jeremy Johnson
Archie & Pat Kutz
Rosemary & Lew Lloyd
Jimmy & Wendy Mnookin
The Northern Poetry Exchange
Boo Poulin ❄ Robert H. Smith
Jerry Vorrasi
George & Bonnie Wallace
David & Ellen Wallack
Thomas R. Ward
Pat & Michael Wilder
Jim Zeman